INDECENCY

INDECENCY

Justin Phillip Reed

COFFEE HOUSE PRESS

Minneapolis

2018

Coffee House Press books are available to the trade through our primary distributor, Consortium Book Sales & Distribution, cbsd.com or (800) 283-3572. For personal orders, catalogs, or other information, write to info@coffeehousepress.org.

Coffee House Press is a nonprofit literary publishing house. Support from private foundations, corporate giving programs, government programs, and generous individuals helps make the publication of our books possible. We gratefully acknowledge their support in detail in the back of this book.

LIBRARY OF CONGRESS CATALOGING-IN-PUBLICATION DATA
Names: Reed, Justin Phillip, author.
Title: Indecency / Justin Phillip Reed.
Description: Minneapolis : Coffee House Press, 2018. | Includes
    bibliographical references.
Identifiers: LCCN 2017039180 | ISBN 9781566895149 (softcover :
    acid-free paper)
Classification: LCC PS3618.E435653 A6 2018 | DDC 811/.6—dc23
LC record available at https://lccn.loc.gov/2017039180

PRINTED IN THE UNITED STATES OF AMERICA
25 24 23 22 21 20 19 18   6 7 8 9 10 11 12 13

CONTENTS

Performing a Warped Masculinity en Route to the Metro   1

Witness to the Woman I Am Not   2

Pushing up onto its elbows, the fable lifts itself into fact.   6

Nothing Was Ever Itself Only   8

Take It Out of the Boy   9

Any Unkindness   10

Portrait with Stiff Upper Lip   11

Slough   12

Anesthesia Is a Country You Leave for America   13

|p|l|e|a|s| 14

The Day _____ Died   15

Gateway   16

About a White City   18

A Statement from No One, Incorporated   25

The Requital   27

Snowfall Throws Its Pretty Noise upon a Weary Sameness   28

How to Keep It Down / Throw It Off / Defer until Asleep   29

On Being a Grid One Might Go Off Of   31

Retrograde   32

Untitled (We aint even posed to be here)   33

Porch Smoke: An Implication in Three Acts   34

I Wish I Knew How It Would Feel   37

On Self-Reliance   38

Consent   39

Exit Hex   40

Orientation   41

Necessary Room   42

To Every Faggot Who Pulverized Me for Being a Faggot   43

Black Can Sleep   45

On Life as an Exercise in Preparing to Die   46

Carolina Prayer   47

Exchange   48

The Leak in This Old Building   51

The Fratricide   52

Theory for Expansion   54

They Speak of the Body and One Sits Up Straight   55

A Victim Dissolves into Tears   56

Paroxysm   58

Notes   69

INDECENCY

i thought the self was a long hand
angling into difficult minutes,
pushing through to arrive more rigid
and crooked in its familiar stance.
i looked on as the thing went loping
mule-hooved past each body raised
war-sharp beside it, decided i'm afraid—
not of every other body slashing moments
in the once-whole morning of my own,
but because the blade is time ripping
selves like shirts to gauze to web. is living
what i observe when left alone
to furtively stare at smudged reflections,
histories flattened—legible as concrete
tunnel as shelter—into contours
against the plexiglas? what question
does the self ask at the body's behest
that time won't wring from the body itself?
i thought that i was a long hand.

WITNESS TO THE WOMAN I AM NOT

(in which all this white is my gaze)

silence's girth. the decorative laurel boughs, zephyr-rascalled twigs crackling in and out of sight, weighing. bow to pick up anything— bobby pin—jackknife into treaty. bend at the knees: waste not. tightly, walk. "slow up, shorty," "ay." sidewalk hooves, acquittal acquittal, the dense streets clapped into a quick-descended stillness.

(in which all this white is my gaze)

the mouth can no longer feel the name in it. deictics stuff the gasp. gash. "and she" "of her" "over there" "well, we" the labial-lingual demand of speech. exit with arrangements: under lights, with full faculties. corral of faces with enemies close. whistle the wet trill.

(in which all this white is my gaze)

in the box heat-seeking the woman i am not: blades. badges. tie clips winking beneath fluorescence. to stitch the story is cauterizing work: words from either whimper swelling to quarantine, to hinder. "is that all you can remember" isn't a question. to expedite the illustration with their tongue-tip familiars: "snatched" and "muffled." flints.

(in which all this white is my gaze)

the dress, a worried mess of splinters, somehow yet a dress.

PUSHING UP ONTO ITS ELBOWS, THE FABLE LIFTS
ITSELF INTO FACT.

after Tafisha Edwards

To disappear Black girls at a low volume of sustained public panic
is to insinuate the inconstancy of Black girls. The disposability of
Black girls who are prone to disappearance. A body bag somewhere
waits with little hoopla about its lot. Absence becomes the lot of
Black girls.

_____ will eventually accept as fact that absence becomes a lot
of Black girls. In what becomes the normal day-to-day, Black girls
are harder to find, _____ would think first, not that there are
few attempts to find them. The question isn't whether Black girls
often go missing. If no one else, Black girls miss each other.

_____ would be remiss to not recognize how everything is
made less in the absence of Black girls, if _____ could miss what
_____ have never been required to recognize, such as:

Unlike missing Black girls, taking Black girls is a Western custom.
It seems likely that such a statement will soon appear inaccurate: the
white space in new textbook editions will have nothing to say about
it, if the white spaces behind those textbooks have anything to say
about it. That Black girls are quintessential American palimpsests is
not a question but an anxiety. _____ would rather forget that
Black girls were made receptacles for what the authors of *Liberty*
and *Independence* would not speak. That *Liberty* and *Independence* were
imaginable only in the absent-presence of taken Black girls, enslaved
Black girls, Black girls on whom a foundational economic system
so depended that white men would kill each other and take taken
Black girls.

The constancy of Black girls is someone's anxiety. The soil is thick with hidden Black girls, the myth that only quiet Black girls are worthwhile Black girls. The soil turns as _____ turn away from loud Black girls and their cacophonic insistence on Black girls.

_____ have not insisted enough upon the fact of Black girls, are often loudly shocked to find Black girls disappeared. Loud, unsustained shock has a way of disappearing Black girls. Outrage, too, has a way of being disappeared.

from another little death sleep i rise to find
the id well hidden and life's slow states of
matter still in place. there are doors here
that almost fit precisely in their frames.
there must be a lukewarm month when
this is more so. the swollen season
trembles on its hinges: i am not ready to
carry the carnal weight. i haven't swept
the welcome mat, haven't taken advantage
of the free counseling sessions, have been
there before. i have the cold palm in my
crotch, reddening, and later i'll hate its in-
sufficience. dust of my flagellation pillows
the prostrating bones; the resting jaws
cleft apart on the firm plane of mattress
let the mouth do its infantile, dumb-wide
appeal.

forget the world's smallness. i'm tired
of pretending. i've been lost. the storeroom
of a hotel pool is approximately the size
of our lives anyway. can't imagine a vault
so black and left to itself. waistband slipping
and him saying "yeah, you always acted like
a white boy." so. so black my elbows
stripe their char on the carpet. so black i
throw it back. so black "you in them guts,
nigga" "daddy" "king." are we convinced?

when you fuck me and i don't
like it, is that violence. you keep
goring my form in pursuit
of an end i have hidden from
even myself. no words are safe—
i have such illusions about s&m
and what pain is not.
when you fuck me and i think
[brutal] is the best word for this
winter, is that normal. i'm not
there under your nails because
you chew them out of habit.
i'm holding your hand so you
can't harm a thing that i pity.
the pinkness of the skin
around the nail is an omen.
brutal is the winter and some days
a bird migration may as well be
any unkindness of ravens. is it
generous to think i'm as malignant
as a sinkhole. is it violent,
hoping we don't think alike at all.
it could kill us, what we don't
know but are starting to glimpse

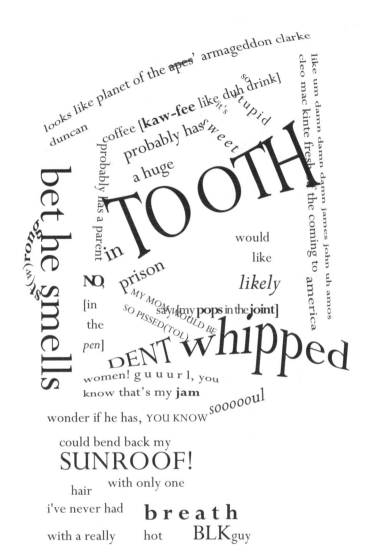

looks like planet of the ~~apes~~' armageddon clarke

duncan

coffee **[kaw-fee** like duh drink]

probably has ~~so~~ ~~it's~~ stupid

probably has a parent s w e e t

a huge

in TOOTH

bet he smells (w)rong

NO,

[in

the

pen]

prison

MY MOM
SO PISSED(TOL)

say [my **pops** in the **joint**]

YOU WOULD BE

would

like

likely

DENT whipped

women! g u u u r l, you

know that's my **jam**

wonder if he has, YOU KNOW sooooooul

could bend back my

SUNROOF!

hair with only one

i've never had **b r e a t h**

with a really hot BLKguy

like um damn damn james john uh amos
cleo mac kinte fresh of the coming to america

SLOUGH

For most of this life I've cultivated
a cosmopolitan fantasy
full of black tile, blood tints, and chrome
fixtures. Have wished to be as lithe as
a hook, slim as a silver antenna.
In the first dream that I remember,
my mother enters an Amoco
for a pack of Newports and doesn't
exit. In the second, I discover
a white man wrapped in white sheets in my bed,
bare chested, and the light blown through
the windows is white, as are the walls:
here is my sex before I could say so.
Here is my wrist where the dream was
flayed off, the scar once as stark and embossed
as railroad laid to make nowhere a place.
I've scrubbed my own maroon out of the porcelain
mouth of a pedestal sink upon
request, forced such distance between
substance and self, slighted evidence
when lies were convenient, and never
kept for myself the insistence
of color. I have outplayed no god.

Anesthesia Is a Country You Leave for America

The tension in a St. Louis suburb following the shooting of an unarmed African American teenager by a police officer was thrown into stark relief Sunday night in a video captured by CNN of a police officer yelling a derogatory phrase at protesters.

"Bring it, all you fucking animals! Bring it!" the officer said in the exchange.

under a weight of slush-rumped bodies
rutting, i drew breath: rancor,
the clamor of their anchors dragging

bottom, having spooned bare
with unchecked decadence my bowl
of raw sugar. at my nape, lips

around an anemic sucking maw
lubed in a just secretion smacked
"but listen" "but still." in the dream

i was blind and white as bone.
i appeared picked not quite clean,
not right until——. the growls

serrated my stirring limbs
with pristine teeth they were before
flesh fell deadish where i slept.

their whole heavy tongue slack
in my own throat, opiate-slow.

|P|L|E|A|S|

what is the word for the realization that your language never loved
you? you are a red thing / scattered, sad map of

       sacrificial fires   nightly appealing

where is that word?

it becomes necessary to signify the passing sound of friends who
swear fidelity to oneself and in the same exchange refuse the weight
of one's brother's body, collapsed and dragged forward by its will
to keep running. it becomes necessary to signify the smear, the oil
of him slicked across blacktop, how at night he disperses in shine
and gas. you think the word is [lapse]: the illusion to which one
clings to keep from being both crazy and american, disrupted. glitch
and pixel—the eternally loading screen that is blackness waiting
to be called other than absence of. lapse / lap, which is—for the
mother—a sign of the child having lived.

maybe your friends cannot exist within the glitch.

there are lapses of justice / of memory / of time before the body is
covered / before those left to mourn lapse into savagery, which the
friends say they (just) cannot abide.

i disavowed "died" but didn't mutter "murdered" in the direction of anyone who uttered it. i collapsed the umbrella of my shoulders into circumflex over a keyboard and clicked away morning. at lunch i was nowhere i could call you back from. there, i munched granola and grew miraculously blacker. my boss's chin tilting collarward kinda meant to mean i matter, but i thought fuck if i'm two cool fingertips to the temples / i'm not fine but uncannily coarse as the mud-eyed jerk-bootied affect of a james brown mug shot / no thanks for the talk no tongues today counting downbeats we can syncopate tomorrow. anyway, the day after would be as gray and guilty as a hardwood-bound heartbeat's corner-cobweb-throbbing echo. i requested a rain check. in the car at five, i crawled outta my business and cranked bass against three busted speakers. i remember there was a road.

GATEWAY

Delmar Boulevard, Saint Louis

winter rain whips you into
cane shape

at the sight, something in you
crawled up

a cop's spine & frisked every
damn where

benches clap on first & fourth
down here

your whole shitty block of trash
built beige

alleyway cardboard cuts out
bodies

heavy with living death, lungs
packing

past a sack of centuries
pant-sag

your own blood hard up drops
black thud

traces yardbird song & thrum
been sad

as miles of revitalized
gravestone

your stuck flash-wide sprawl, liver
gored on

your rouged-cotton infant coos
cribside

the watershed: alarms all
curtsied

with bass in the waists of your
daughters

no rhythm no blues but
dumpsters

cute cubicles like kennels
boxed up

your glare-proof pickets protest
big lip

service to a tranquil re-
public

bleating guilt, panhandle &
pout-suck

off your tempered glass, your cured
blond grass

sound's nostalgia you curate
boneless

sinking teeth deep in safe codes
gating

your high-stakes crown, your goodness
glue-clung.

About a White City

after James Schuyler

The barren ground feels
the dead pressed
into a long distraction
of asphalt.

You pile the less
pleasant bits of news
easily through all the sleep
and line the story of years.

It's too long,
turning and
turning upon itself.

A thick pain—
what precisely happened
years / days /
hours ago.

That blue night, cut with red.

Heavily, you wait.

The forced future is just
more fight all the time.
So much dirt and laundry.
Blood sponged easily off the day.

It seems
calculatedly malevolent:

Terrors threaded by hands
undo another day
gray with use.

A door slams. Someone
goes as far as the shop
and in the fullness of time
you empty a glass of whiskey.

How many boys?
Make a list, learn
their names,

forget them.
They were here, now
they're not. Rope
tied to a tree and head

in the muddy creek.
What a long time it seemed
rising to the surface.

Is repetition boring?
Quite a few things go nowhere
and back.

Another day,
a friend calls. Another,
a redder red
than blood gathers

and sets on its edge
the mind. It rains again:
a breakdown occurs,

something like eating
the pattern of many moods
naked in winter.

Time heals

what? The rotting
will surely cement and leave you
too much too often.

Streaking trails of violet light
the wet street reflects
a rim of moon

and bursts into tears.
The snow
brushed gray-black with mud.

The deep art of these days.

The city rears up:
white, white, lovely.
Inside, every room
mutates like a basic truth.

They say there are those
who have never
felt terror. How fine.

A couple passes,
jogging. Fine.

The world coasts by
unexpected, mysterious,
or running, or simply lying.

An old man at the store
rattles with catarrh,
is rough, caught
untranslatable,
subjective, an idle
thought,
          a racket.

Ordinary household
pain is a freight. A bus
passes with its burden
of need.

What is that chatter?

The matter of business:
a rug, underneath which is swept
the living dirt. Go.
Hasten. Tarry. Bluest
eyes and bird tongues crash
at the restless surface,
chewing and spitting and and
and all this without thought.

The men are machines. The white
engine assembles a sincere
crack in the silence.
This churning sucks up the day.
The violent muck is quite other.

Crooked branches lift admissions to the horrors.

A month of dust. You
want to cling to being,
want to go before the snap
and still press your face into
the life mask.

                What happens now

wide and mindless impermanence

A new shop is being built,
an old one refurbished. A white
interior, changes in taste.

But there is your face.
You reluctantly open up
and hang out. Visitors
misunderstand silence

for approval. You stir
abstractions and generalities.
The evening seems set.

The truth, daily work.

The past is

suddenly ahead.

Stand it

            it utters questions.

"what is it when a death is ruled a homicide but no one is responsible for it" ——Hanif Abdurraqib

A Statement from No One, Incorporated

We are not responsible. We have not
the capacity to respond, cannot take
your call, are not obliged. We promise
nothing in return except that we will
return, asking that the potential profit
this lost life's labor could have produced
be accounted for, and blaming our
Black dead president for the deficit. We
are deficient and without your damage
the world is difficult work to live on.
We live on the unanswerable, assert
that acknowledgment is inartistic,
history is regressive, and aggression
looks like no one we know. No one
is responsible while we have the luxury
to see ourselves as infinite ones, ocean
of individual possibility. We are so
many blades in the yard the wind
runs screaming invisibly through.
We need to have a deeper dialogue
about the need for deeper dialogue,
but oh oh, we are always these spondees
of speechlessness and cannot process
your request, are too busy about
our dreams. The celestial bodies appear
from here, ripe for colonies and more
questions. We are over earthly inquiry
and unfortunately, though your sigh
traveled light-years from the dark
matter of gravity we're intrigued to find

you now are, we will not see you today
(we are recessed on narrowing beaches,
toasting our gods with a wellsprung red
we cannot source but are confident
the year was relatively good), but here,
for your trouble, for coming so far:

"they" "how could they how could they how could" the wrench turns, stripping the bolt's predictable angles to soft exposure— which is the week and which is the mind? what of the fine residual powder's threat of lockjaw from the throat's u-bend? an exhale. one gives up on fitting into language. there *is* a "they" the day endorses. from its perch on the dog-ear picket the finch shits and doesn't look down. one wonders if it's the same bird that has daily laid its dry white waste on the storm door handle. one enters, lingers in the vesica piscis of public-private with a last glance at landscape (brick, rail black, a motorcade of leaves), leaves the city like a friend at the window. one commences the mime of self-love:

disrobing the

dangling routine in the

obligatory uncoupling of the parts

SNOWFALL THROWS ITS PRETTY NOISE UPON A WEARY SAMENESS

The debt collection mail in columns. I keep trying
not to smoke or smoke again or smoke so much
but fuck it. The grandfather is dying. It's obvious how
the planet has been inching for a century toward this.

On the phone my mother's voice assumes a new
alien edge. As if through the blades of a fan, it asks
the usual, "How's my baby doing." This distracts.
I'm a digression in the day's essay pushing her to

its imminent stop. She's taking a week off from work
she says. I don't believe the brackets framing her
assurance in this moment. Someone should acknowledge
how impossible this notion of doing is becoming

but I'm not the one. I lie. I do nearly anything not
to hear her speak into a wind at [okay]'s precipice.
Her words and mine just blow a commotion of iotas
massing embankments we can neither incinerate nor eat.

How to Keep It Down / Throw It Off / Defer until Asleep

My stomach imagines itself as an injury.
I steep ginger-mint tea in the
inauguration memorabilia mug from Momma,
monument-white but for Obama.
Between self-harm and my hand, I've rigged a list
of reliable illusions. This is the first
gesture. I am a gentle fist. My body
has been deboned of its irony.
My life wants to be proven
to. I didn't check the list of Black church dead in Charleston
for friend or cousin
because this morning it was Thursday. Work was quiet
after I asked a white girl if she could quit
whispering—the hissing hit

his reddest venous notes until
a droning rain applauded. His ears ring full
of answers to his own knocking
when he's home alone—i.e., almost always. Pacing
the apartment for a nest in which to
knuckle shut and wax unknown, he
statues and envisions
both spread hands rooting a brown expanse
into the kitchen floor's glaucous linolcum,
and after, the image on Instagram
with heightened contrast, hashtagged *emblem*
etc, and producing this proof
would require one of his hands, and what if—
Nearby in the drying rack, a knife

shines. Impetuous.

And it occurs to you that this

occurring to you is a thinner ice

than most other Thurs-

days, is skin quickly shucked off a winter's

lip. The hour itself murmurs

open better yet back like a hang

nail, as in persistent rawness and in the wrong

direction. You hunker the mug sternumwise—

it's hot as a kind of heart meat but a blanched blues

—and mother your torso around it like a

matryoshka

mold, chest sickled over the steaming vent

that is the President's head, though you pretend it isn't.

On Being a Grid One Might Go Off Of

The first step is to stop just beyond the weight of organs.
The sense of gravity sitting in tissue is like the space between
carcass and curb, before the reek worms into rock pores:
a sleeplessness there, that continual niche-thrash. You too

once knew what it was to feel impressive. As the bed dissolves
into the walls, the walls disrobe themselves of their edges
and your resolve is now acute in the locking jaw of darkness.
Beg to be let. You, like bravery, leave behind the breath-inflated

lump, its depths, and its refusal to lace the cells of scars over even
the metaphorical guttings. To manage the act exceeds the box-
and-whisker of lately's along-going. You've grown so accustomed
to mereness that what you call a life no longer houses the sublime.

It seems easy to leave. It seems this easy to leave. After
a second you'll want to consider the centimeters of resistance
stitching air between here and all of elsewhere. But, still,
inhabit the bodiless second. To possess it is a bearable joy.

the upstairs neighbor makes you think you've gone soft in the brain. you yell GODDAMMIT in the dark; an audience of one responds: a sigh, upheaved from your own intestinal waiting room. at four a.m. his cowboy boots resume assaulting floorboards, screeching inches above your ceiling tiles, which have the consistency and the weak promise of white cake. some nights he descends to the basement to do his girlfriend's laundry. you feel invaded while the metal dryer shudders on the concrete slab. the angry black words on the brain's page flash first **oppressive** then **encaged** and **would ~~if i had a gun~~ blow a hole through a surface between us to remind him i'm alive down here and hate to be alone with myself so close to others.** his fucking seems inconsiderate when it runs over the sleep-aid playlist you made in desperation because—and this is key—the neighbor is also a friend. and kind. two years the two of you have kept a decent social contract, sort of a good-and-service trade involving tylenol, wireless internet, and transportation when your car again has given you its ass to kiss. and yet who you are isn't smothered enough by the civil superego not to hate his grunts of understatement, her button-track ohgods, and the vacuous erection now making controversy of your spinal-wire tangle.

a barrier in denim and leather, you warm your boots up near the flames. a babble of inside jokes and costly pleasantries crests and wanes. the (white) (english) friend would like this seat next to you, which you were / are saving. wait, see: aren't there other places for him to sit around the fire pit? in the 43-degree night, there is one: stool, steel, elevated, awkward. why can't he—but why couldn't you have—he is sitting. it is a cold communal adhesive between you.

you haven't been doing well: deluding yourself in trying to erect a system equally as formidable as that which always outlies your terrifying / terrified body. your presumption of antagonism— the wind-raw season of it—hardens into a condition. you (are) assume(d). you (are) position(ed).

you cannot raise such ambiguous walls as those inside the bar. harriet tubman frowns down from one, permanently framed in her negation. her mouth is a ∪ on its head. that ∪ symbolizes intersections of events in probability and statistics. jackie wilson is lonely teardropping up from a speaker, and one of you is doubling whiskeys, and another one of you just walked in the door. you cannot turn and say "sorry, but no, the (brown) man who sits here on the bench is ~~like~~ my brother." you can only be tired of moving against. you know, you can be so tire(d)some(times).

PORCH SMOKE: AN IMPLICATION IN THREE ACTS

I.

it is may. naturally, there are rabbits that barely move but for breathing, hunched among the high weed patches, spaced so they can't be kept in a single gaze.

ONE *sees each left eye*	*suspect*
ears stonestill, upright	*cocked*

there are rabbits. and over the fence are BMWs *and the double bleeps of alarm systems arming. (mis)hearing "we see you" in the mere opening of doors and fearing the confines of* you,

the MICROAGGRESSED MODE *retaliates in monosyllables:*
> you are a you too / hell you are more you than i / now i see
> you / **who** the fuck are **you** / who **are** you

the cat-curious brewery patron wives, purse-clutching and wide-berthing and breathing, string you *up in the mid-city scenery to be recalled in later regalia: "was a little edgy."*

II.

hacked off and scattered: ONE *conceives a cradle in the sentiment.*

perpendicular to the litter of dead grass, the blackbirds march a combing front across the yard. they dart / stab their plot into newly uniform green, feast on the yielded slithering nudes. ONE *fields a grief behind the eye blinked unglazed.*

proposes the AUGURING MODE*:*

> what stripped, steaming waste the great mirroring empty on wings will lay

on cue, the ready pen and synapses threaten to coincide these wracks. (a note about blocking:

dis/ tract/ dis/ associate)

> there will always be things. they will always rise unbelievably quickly.

III.

evening:

SOMEBODY'S MAMA *across the alley yells at the dog* / *child the threat*
> come back her(e) right nah(w)
> (*garbled expletives*)

a violence is sure to ensue. ONE *reckons with the approach of a moment in*
which the mouth can reproduce with accuracy
> everything, officer

and
> not shit

a rude crow murder circles with no coordinates——*sky scabs. their blue-black*
staccato choral [are] [are] [are]s terrify in their insistent noncommittal.

ALL MODES *move indoors.*

a wasp's nest of white men begins at daybreak
to break down and busy up the house next door
I hear them drone in my dead sleep hammering
my head against the brick chest of a bright morning
outside one heaves his whole belly beneath
a box full of toilet and another in the road yells
gotdamn his back hurts just watching and there's
a hole in the street beside him and inside that
another white man and don't you know
I don't care who he is or where he'd rather be
or how hungry his ragamuffins or how fucked up
his own toilet I want that hole to shut
him up and the asphalt to lick its lips and that
I don't care what wanting this makes me
looks like what they've called freedom I want
these holes in my back shut up I want the dead
boy inside me to bury white men alive yes
all of them in his gut I snap the teeth of my blinds
down because don't I know every white man
has a dead black child inside him bursting
with the desire to materialize in the street
as a manhole I want to keep someone safe I say
I used to feel safe and don't mean it I say
if I eat them all I am a cradle for
cradles but if I eat them all I am also just
a city full of white men I am sick with
revitalization I am such a sepulchre
if I eat them they will still be busy busy busy
as a virus trying to keep me alive just as long
as my body is the gracious host for their
buildup which you know has been
the longest breakdown gotdamn
I say it too my back hurts just knowing
what they wish it would still do

nobody knows who one is and
the texture of knowing this
doesn't feel human. one says
these things aloud.

the daily affiliations collude as
allergens around the sleeping head.
one wakes and within minutes is
again a friend / brother / son /
student / teacher / debtor / eater,
wishing authenticity would crawl
in teleprompter lines ascending
violet over the eyes.

the dishes spill a war of effort
from the sink, across the counter.
the coffeemaker's under siege.

the disconsolation of being mass-
produces the placebo of semantics
without quota or switch. "can't
you fucking shut it off" each word
subsists in the guts of others. one
bottles them all and becomes
a container of supplements—

"but why won't he want me"
"why won't he just want me"
"why won't he want just me"

now he's pushing himself up into. a life into time.
a once in a life that is gathering speed—his point
to prove—is swiftly becoming a not-just-once.
the knot of you, rescinding. out of you, pouring,
the product of a swallowed "i don't want to
anymore," which feels to him like a welcoming slick.
damn the skin crying its quicksilver at his slither,
the rapid breath that can't believe it's expected
to be unbelieving again. he's into a groove that
is darkly reminiscent of crossways and rolling stops:
"what do you like to do" into "how soon can i come
over" into "address," and now, out of sheath out of
sheath comes the sound of you scrawling into time,
sheath, a myth of how this was an incident like any
other; and for you, what's the truth if not that.
knot of you, fraying away from what's felt. how
the home you've made from the hollow nasal
innards of "i want" is still a moan out of.

EXIT HEX

for Rogan Hardy

Twice I've turned my head to see a cop

inside me find himself in love. His thumb

heavy in the novel of my body kept my spine

from snapping shut. I fucked and found myself

while following the bullet to its logical conclusion.

Girl, I guess there's glamour in it. Night slid

the street lamp's haloed cantaloupe behind me

behind him while I fondled my keys. One hole

in my skull pulled through the plum sky Mars's light.

ORIENTATION

after Rashid Johnson

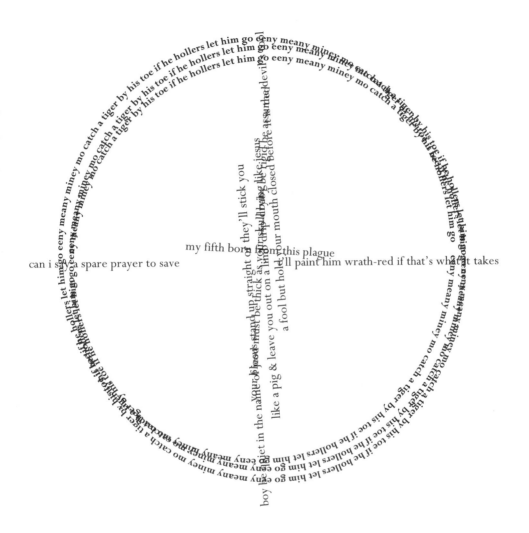

the virulence: "faggot" evolves, a freight-
resistant strain. i cut the day into paltry
fractions spent preparing to retort and
defend the ego against contrivances of
vocal cord, dental ridge, glottal stop,
passing wind. relent to damage: hackles as
debris, contracted brow as gauge. a
colloquial "cocksuckers" issues—what does
mean then mean? the minute's leaving un-
intersected. senselessly the thing grin(d)s:
his mouth continues to mechanize. mouth
torquing my shadow-bound mind must be
removed from context: mouth now
cropped square out of its ocular scene

TO EVERY FAGGOT WHO PULVERIZED ME FOR BEING A FAGGOT

You were right to tell yourself
you'd never live this. You wouldn't
have survived. Each time my carpal flex
flashed open and stained whatever
clean appliance—rim of tub, my own
teeth where I sucked the wound quiet—
with its rouge run-off, I watched you
run off. I've told that story. I've taken a look
at the slow sea monster of my vomit
luminous in the toilet bowl, two digits
of my fingers still slick, nearly
erotic with gag slime: there was
my cocktail of daily medicine, half
digested. There was a line of folk
ready to tell me Black men don't do this
to themselves. They don't, you said,
take dick either, but here I am. There
you are. Some night I was so hungry and tired
and high on my prescription, I let
a man I didn't know feed me vodka
and orange juice until I would remember
neither my dreams nor his hands.
In three of the five psych wards I nested in
like a nomad bird—because where else
could I rest—I fell in love easily. I once stepped
entirely into a bottle of pills and tried to screw
my body finally underground. My father
lifted me seizing into a hospital and out
of his house shortly thereafter. Dear fellow
gay-ass nigga, who loves you these days?
I hope it's Black people. I hope no one
stole the certainty of that away from you.

To believe that white men had my back
was a facile act: who else so long
prepared to help me hate me?
I've told this story. I barely graduated.
I stunted my own growth. I don't know how
to go home. What you don't know is
I needed someone like you but braver. Now
I just have issues with needing anyone at all.
Your wife is shrugging out of a nightgown
and sinking under sheets. There are
drippings of me still between
your teeth. You've since taken
men in your mouth and said a silent
word to God. You could lie
there beside her wholly without conflict
or bitterness. She could be he. They
could be happy and the world
in which I've learned I live no less itself.
From its stubborn clay I've shaped
a creature, hollowed into its guts
a pair of lungs, attached appendages
that make it capable of walking
out of every room it enters at will
and willed it to love. What have you done.

Black Can Sleep

on a nail bed. Black be
quick as catch can. Corner
hanger-on, black a dead
cell waiting to low-ceiling its empty
belly down a mop-dragged floor.
Lure of draining, black goes
to ground. Rain dangles: black hitches
like hick cargo. Call round. There it is
a thumb in the milk, trunk junk
strewn across a killing
of lilies. Oh Lord,
black the valley. Wise men
slather mirth, lip the gum. The news
their black tomb of tooth sucks out
won't news. Black know: Pops
a stone stopped quiet
(of all sounds) in the rolling.
Black cancer. Black sugar.
Black pressure. Black taken
off support's hollow leg. Use
to be an hour visited
on us, stained Colt & wild
around the neck, ex
of auntie, blackest one yet,
picked up only after zip,
pockets just a snatch of *ay*

young black, how you live?

when once again you won't make it home in order to confirm, you imagine the aunt's large body (which is so much of who she was to you and why you rarely perceived her without a cast or crutch or patient's bracelet) with its many secret, unsexual creases, compactly folded—ceremoniously, like a handkerchief or spotted gauze—into the coffin.

does the mind conjure forth for the scene a scent? you think you wouldn't recognize formaldehyde, nor would any undertaker with a budget for carnations allow the smell to linger. there's a reason it is the funeral flower. as well, *carnation* once referred to the color of flesh: beyond the black and white meats, the bloody organs arrange a bouquet of crushed roses, paling and exhausted.

you think you know everyone you love will be reduced to somatic allegory, and that knowing so is key to persisting—how you can, during the horror film, control the heart's response by recalling where this or that knife strike will fall. the monster-killer will appear in the medicine-cabinet mirror. the flesh will tear like drenched paper.

Carolina Prayer

Let the blood if your belly must have it, but let it
not be of me and mine. Let my momma sleep.
Let her pray. Let them eat. Let the reverend's
devil pass over me. Let the odds at least
acknowledge us. Let the breasts be intact,
the insulin faithfully not far, and let the deep
red pinpoint puddle its urgency on a pricked
fingertip. Let the nurse find the vein the first time.

Let the kerosene flow and let my grandma praise
her bedside lord for letting her miss another winter.
Let me be just a little bit bitter so I remember:
Your columns and borders aint but the fractured,
the broke clean, the brownest gouges in the blades
of our great-great-great shoulders. Let me leave
and come back when my chest opens for you wider
than your ditches did to engorge my placeless body.

The mosquito-thick breath in your throat coats my skin
and it almost feels as if you love me. Let the AC
drown out the TV. Let the lotion bottle keep a secret
corner til Friday. Let Ike, Wan, D-Block, all my brother's
brothers ride through the weekend. Let the cop car
swerve its nose into night and not see none of them.
Let us smell rain. Let the breeze through an oak hymn
the promise that keeps us waking. Let the cicada
unwind while hushpuppy steam slips out the knot
of a tourist's hand, and let him hear in it legends
of how hot grease kept the hounds and the lash at bay.

Exchange

my mother extends an arm with options: beating, or
        punishment. i consider, this early, a thrashing
        patience. dilemma of immediate or pending lack.

leather belt gives to buttocks red welts, some fleeting
        eternities. the throat throws back evidence of first
        effect. the mind threads the sting into memory /
        inhibition / correlation. the bathtub's cold lip
        becomes a body to embrace. i pray for reprieve,
        numb convection. i try to enter. i still cannot leave.

*

my bae sleeps folded into my lap. if i cling to him, does it make me
more or less of a top? a subordinate clause? which position privileges
parataxis? in what design do i hold power? he falls asleep first and
easily. the unbothered comma of him emasculates me, a sheep-count
neurosis i never admit to anyone.

*

the drag shop cashier says "you should sit every chance you get"

"your legs look amazing" says momma

"that halloween outfit was everything"

"these heels hurt, though. how do you all-damn-day hurt?" i mean
       "for whom do you hurt?"

            *

no man appraises my body in the way [i] appraise my sister's body
as she hikes it farther away. she pools and it spills and she rises and
it runs through us all and collects dry lips at its edges, sipping and
lifting and swilling her round

to where / with whom / into what / which he / which he

no eye flies over my sister's body and wants as [i] want to contain
it, and this invokes a synonymy: to protect and to devour.
in my mouth her best interest is no different from fleeing a
kingdom until i'm far enough to claim dominion on the other
side. the scenery is the same. the [i] thought it knew better

        *

what the young divorcé means to do with me
has nothing to do with me, our nights suggest.
he says his ex-wife's fault was that "she just
didn't try." his ex has nothing to do with me.

his teeth convene in the snarl of an otherwise
canine as we roll our kill across the carpet,
singeing. the friction is convincing. he likes that
we don't like each other enough to lose

anything. we try extracting maximum
play from minimum utterance, grunting
and sleeping til one night i dream of being
the moon-necked wife annoyed at the mess of him,

so we quit fucking and the door to elsewhere
                                        opens me like a cut.

                    *

time, as trained, blackens the belt's kiss. my skin
        does not remember what exactly it misses. it tends
        to confuse whom it was said once to belong to, oddly
        relates the sting to being known, the body heat like
        humiliation. a shame is avoidance of physical pain.

love later debuts as rasping sob, sometimes as surprise
        blow to the torso. once there was the man who before
        he died hoisted me high with one arm while thwacking
        my flailing thigh with the other. i should have begun
        there. my mother's force is a kind of overpour.
        in the way of apologies, we have little to say.

The Leak in This Old Building

as a toddler my brother learns to answer a bricklayer uncle:

"what ladies like"   "suga suga"
"what mens like"   "hugs"

—a smeared sweet on his cheek in the parenthesis of a grin

I was coerced into my brother's murder. Because I loved him I was made to live for him. Inside him. As him. Drowned him in a solution of bathwater, bleach, and shredded pages. Watched his brown prune, watched the steam pirouette, the hostage blood beating at the doors of his palms. My eyes teared beneath the fumes. His eyes retreated with history's entirety. I scissored through the chemistry hissing his skin loose. I peeled away the glove though it snagged

at the nail. I stopped to admire the pristine muscles built by some thousand signatures. I spread the batwings over his pecs, flipped him and lifted the coriaceous back flesh. I said it looked nothing

you look at how his
look at how his face
look at how his face
look at his face still
look at his face **how**
at his face **how can**
his face **how can**
how can you still

like a saddle, leaving the rust diamond of his trapezius to flicker. I cut away the whole taxed shadow of Blackness but left the pouch around his sex, which at last belonged to him alone. The rest dangled, drying on a wire. There was a full-tilt river where the droplets fell. I was already wearing the skin of his skull, molding its contours to mine. The brown irises peering out were neither of ours. I shaped our lips to form the word "breathe" and coughed a ghost. I glimpsed him in a mirror and was lost in his hair. The dense serpentine net, stitching both of us closed. My own life still stuck there, a wad of fist and teeth. \

You tongue us in a single slippage. You total it "he" / "they" / "one" / "and the other one" / "Sorry, was that you." You swear it was he. You're sorry, sorry, sorry. We look different on paper. We seem different fingerprinted. You met us last week, but it's good to meet again. Hi, you're Caitlyn. Kelly. Katy. With a C. Cathy with long hair. Jennifer, long hair. Jenny for short. Tom with two Ms, no H. You have a brother with our name. Your uncle's middle initial helps you remember which. // No proactive effort to practice cataloging the white body. It is blond / brunette / sandy / auburn / amber / hazel / olive / freckled / Irish / Jewish /

face   can   still   not
can   still   not   **you**
still   **can   you   not**
how   can   you   not
can   you   still   not
you   still   not   look
you   still   not   look   at
not   look   at   his   face

German-Irish / Italian / maternally Hungarian. The eyebrows give it away. // Which of us read this poem. Thank him. Not him. No, but thanks anyway. Are we brothers. Aren't we our brother. No, but anyway, thanks. We should cut our hair. How can you tell us apart. We should cut our hair. How can we tell ourselves apart for you. How can we help you to tell us apart. How can we help you to tell us apart. How can we help you to tear us apart. How can we help you. You tear us apart. How can we tear us. You help us apart. You help us part. How can we tear you. How can we tear you. How can we help us to tear you apart.

THEORY FOR EXPANSION

considering Michael L. Johnson

At first: indecisive happening, a moment's
incubation, a budding in the rift before this

emergence. Grace-panic. Warhorseman,
spilt. Among sectile bodies, I think of you

*

in succorless hollow. The man you wore
dwindles, wilts unhollered, daggered

inches deeper into cinder block while
the cellblock's every kneecap after knuckle

blesses your flesh dry of betrayal, its raw
use. Your marrow mills its own language

like a system of silkworms, everywhere
utter and sheer—a body behaving

as will any dialect, lifting stranger and more
urgent mouths to the same sentence.

the public doesn't know what to think   of you, spook faggot. it
doesn't think of you   that way. you lie ass-up   on the slab
of its mind, the image a mote   passing tacitly out of light, less than
dead weight, though   you are surely dying   as if
dying is your duty   to country.   spook.   you queen out
on main streets   of ghost towns, sword-dancing   prototype
propelled   toward doom: black   puddle bordered in the sketch of
ancient deaths—floatless,   diminutive,   exoskeletal residua—
still life of body with   circumference of bodies—; puddle   reflecting
nothing of use   to a milk-dipped narcissus.   skull of faggot
in the alley, blown   purple on the bricks,   is a kiss, is a   KS
lesion.   gun hot on the lips   like lips. fucked   as gender.
fucking to live. fucking   appalling. the public   pales
and pales you   like   meat in the wolf maw, snatches   the tongue
out   from under and dresses   its windows in your shade. spook,
what is your color   scheme? faggot: floral printed in fist   blood
bloom.   spook: bullet riddled, sifting   air   overhead for clues.
what's black   and red   and red   all over?   the public
drops   its hand   from the ear where it had   what it thought
was the decency   to whisper.

laughed, "so (i am more into white guys, but)
  i left him   a quiet smile
                 through the glass,   him still there,
and it occurred to me that he was
(gorgeous,   great legs,   well-endowed.)
      a criminal   , brother   the wrong
                     cake
      . he hadn't been chasing me at all
       . i hadn't understood much of what he had said,
   (only my third black guy)
only that he
(asked, '   ?' and he said, '   .' and i was like,
'   fuck   me ' i got   him several
times, and   he)
          was a trick of some kind. he gave the
impression
far deeper than   his words. perhaps i was
   the   escape   route   but
what had *he* to fear?   he
    had   that   long   long
  effect
    he had   to remain unseen and effective.
     what   was   i
     hurt ing   a blackface
      ghost   the white   shot up around
   him.   i knew
(i knew they were clean by looking at them).
         he only wanted
  something. everybody wanted   to use
          me   let him (i let him
come in me)   . i   feeling
   satisfaction   dismissed him so completely.
   it was   dark   i

(with people i barely)
know   was   bending
                       warm   for all his
            return   not
even   i felt
                                           eyes   on   us
      i thought   it ended and
                  now   what an awful   m   he called
                                   often   such things occur
(he calls me and he said, '   disease.')
      what would he say   ? he was far from   being
                       hell   he knew
            better   i
                             i
                       feel better. i   imagine
being   helpless   i
                  i had   to
                                   ('")

Paroxysm

The men in the video fuck facedown.
No, the men on the screen are
faceless, devised to be known

as achronic illustrations of a dare:
the dark organ enters antimatter
and attempts to retain a narrative there.

Bent over the arm of a couch, under
a body you called by a pseudonym
once, you try to ignore the painter's

tarp hanging from the ceiling, the thumb
he keeps resting in his mouth—
minor deviations from the paradigm—

until the only condom goes dry with
the last dregs of lubricant and the scene
resumes its linear obligation to death.

Distorted across another screen
is the latest autopsy of Ezell Ford's
body rendered in diagram, a line

through each wound; the wounds records
of just how many ways
a person can suffer the word

[through]. For a second, you realize
that every single man in the room
has his back to another. Suppose

this were not true all the time.

A feeling in which the rest of the world is a white couple riding horses down the spine of a beach at dusk: there are days upon days of this. You cannot help but assume the eyes behind their shades have only ever cried over sunsets in Venice. It seems that the horses drag the knots of their ankles through surf and are blessed enough to forget they only exist in this labored capacity.

The dead are becoming legion, and those in closest proximity to living shuffle dumbly past in the longest-ever commercial break. This is a show they feel generous enough to admit they cowrote and produced and now can't bear to tune into. Nightly in the cold open a character is assassinated, and you wonder if you won't eventually play the part of every prone body, because no one looks long enough to notice any difference. Maybe it isn't just you, but anyway all your low-resolution murder scenes look the same, says a critic.

If there is a spirit it wishes the body would impose.

You arrive at the university and stand out like a necrotic thumb. Hundreds of future leaders of your free world go out of their way to swim around you and you want to strip naked as a slave and scream DON'T I STINK OF BLOOD but you don't do this because you've been told to think an invisible "we" needs you in this space. You look for proof of your being there. You wonder why Edvard Munch's screaming figure isn't as black as the day is long. No one will say they saw you come in alive.

as when
a child mimics
the sounds of gunfire
so precisely all our bodies
clutch earth

The moment is wry with erotics: in the police, a desire to end resistance, but in that must lie a certain urge toward the end of policing—which you can't believe. The theory refutes itself like a hand in a slamming door. The stubborn complexity of people overwhelms. A rigid fluidity. What do you know.

Your posture's an entire cast of players. You have as many lines as muscles flexing. Say that. It's not as if you cast your faggot shadow like a cloak against the curb. It was a coughing motion. You contract into a spring-load, a choreography of Black proof.

Someone lobs a piece of street through glass. The orifice it makes: a gaping green eye. The unguarded jewelry boutique becomes a wailing feminine parody. Whatever cavalry would come already is here, nightsticking pavement, tattooing its music on you.

the first man you ever loved throws his voice like a plate: up.

the creed blasts into tanks, barracks, linen-shirted veterans,

the thinned-out woodland around, echoes off his darker skin

a duller throb. you stand under sun, salt creased and awful, horn,

clapper, and not understanding. their chorus declares your brother's

prepared to deploy, engage, and destroy your unnamed enemies.

you believe them and cannot unlearn how betrayal became you,

want to shield him from the cheek kiss his allegiance will lay

in place of his face. lately you think the weight of blackness

on his back is a fly's brief landing on a hair's breath, is not

the same stone on your ribs. your citizenship explains away

his   body's   melting   into   this   parading   assembly—

a   noble,   molded   scepter.   your   mouth   is   full   of   bees.

the   flag,   like   a   crimson   lesion,   grins   in   the   wind.

he pivots away on the thirsty field. you begin clocking his steps.

The voice that is warning you constantly against
this clearly wasteful epoch—all
the bees and the oceans and Look What We've Done—
has uttered nothing yet about
your panic: how this one and this one—you learn
despite your will to live to speak

their names in the style of Homeric head counts,
an ocean of their bodies, beached—
were also of this world. They didn't return.
You're asking, "Have you seen them? Are
there rooms in your blueprint of Eden for these
to come to?" And you haven't stopped

debating how weather can matter to you.
Why dam the funnel? Why preserve
any ecosystem incidental
to this incremental disappearance?
The question of living becomes one of
committing to your own extinction.

The apex predation, the brilliance in it,
this global verdant climb beyond—
Is this what it means to be lost in the night?
A paranoir. Unearthing tombs
and slipping inside of annullable memory.
You don't expect survival but

demand to survive nonetheless and believe
as if an afterlife—as if
an extant black mouth will be your legacy.

blood like wine | the ecstatic occasion

for which

there goes the head | against the shield | beyond that | the smiling
toe of a boot

there goes the knee to the back | of the neck

the gloves touching | the cuffing

and many hands, then two | in the crook, uprighting you

here is a complicated discipline

like a father's—isn't it?—love

and a hundred mother | tongues somewhere | darken | and writhe
in | silence

behind the white knuckles of teeth

a mirror | of wrists—inverted prayer | comma of the bladed
shoulder

and arm imitating an alate | withdrawal of effort

the body's simulacrum | of a bullet in slipstream

before the swarm opens its mouth

that folding

When the Black officer searches you,
his is the threadbare habit of having
another man in one's hands. You are
conscious of fucking's metaphor slipping
its dark head through this ajar door
as when, once a year, your father hugs you.
There is in any moment an urge toward
departure. So many shadows here add to
the weight of intimacy's end. When
the Black officer searches your pockets,
a chain rakes across a wall. A splitting
of keys into stars, your night-dragged gut
full of bodies, brine, and waste. What are
the present-tense parts of the present? [weapon]
[the][onyx][juts][crudely][past][ouch][however]

~

you know that the night did not fall. it was dropped.

the evidence is yet uncollected.

the onomasticon in the mind makes room:

a round of hangman.

you eat the salience of waiting,

inhale it, and teeter as a reed in wind at shore—

an indication of the will to move. (god, blow.)

a lamp / some star / vigil romancing the ripples,

a fox-quick pungency of burning wicks.

say it will emerge like a body from a lake,

gasping. splashes, flurry of upset geese.

say it will emerge like a body—

for what were you last destroyed?

for what did you last destroy?

"Pushing up onto its elbows, the fable lifts itself into fact.": Read also Tafisha Edwards's poem "EVERYWHERE IN THE WORLD THEY HURT LITTLE BLACK GIRLS."

"Nothing Was Ever Itself Only": The title is from Carl Phillips's poem "Little Dance Outside the Ruins of Unreason," in his book *The Tether* (New York: Farrar, Straus and Giroux, 2001).

"Anesthesia Is a Country You Leave for America": The epigraph quotes a *Huffington Post* (online) article, "Police Officer Caught on Video Calling Michael Brown Protesters 'F***ing Animals,'" by Amanda Terkel, posted August 12, 2014.

"About a White City" is a liberal erasure and rearrangement of Schuyler's "Hymn to Life."

"Untitled (We aint even posed to be here)": This parenthetical is a line borrowed from Jay-Z's "Niggas in Paris" but not intended to be a precise transcription. About the *aint* here and elsewhere: I omit the apostrophe, first and foremost, in defense of *aint* as a word unto itself. Grammatically, the apostrophe signifies omission, but I begin to question what exactly is omitted. I grew up in a place where *aint* can be deployed effectively in place of *isn't, aren't,* and *am not;* yet the word, as I know it, aint recognizably a contraction. The inclusion of an apostrophe in *aint* often carries, for me, an irreverence of its precise functions and a connotation of lack where (aside from the lack the word itself denotes) there is none.

"Exit Hex": Rogan Hardy is an alias of the porn actor known for "Harlem Hookups."

"Orientation": The poem's shape is inspired by Johnson's sculpture, *Black Steel in the Hour of Chaos,* which shares its title with the 1988 Public Enemy song.

"A Victim Dissolves into Tears" is an erasure of two texts. One is chapter 13 of Ralph Ellison's *Invisible Man.* The other is Steven Thrasher's *BuzzFeed* article, "How College Wrestling Star 'Tiger Mandingo' Became an HIV Scapegoat," posted July 7, 2014. "Tiger Mandingo" is the social media (and better-known) alias of Michael L. Johnson, who was a student at Lindenwood University in the Saint Louis suburb of Saint Charles. Lindenwood coaches recruited Johnson to the university's wrestling team, on which he became a star athlete under the moniker "Tiger." Elsewhere in his life, Johnson took home "Butch Queen" trophies from his loincloth-clad walks in underground drag balls, where he assumed for himself the surname "Mandingo." These identities, referencing Johnson's physical appeal, fueled his popularity on apps like Instagram and Grindr, where he drew the attention of other local gay men cruising for casual sex. I first heard of Johnson while watching the nightly news with my ex-boyfriend. One night a story broke about a Black student who had knowingly infected several men with HIV. In this narrative, Johnson was guilty of borderline premeditated murder. In the mug shot the reporters showed, his face was grim, his skin dry, his hair long and knotty; the effect was terrifying even to me, as I simultaneously distrusted and found myself disgusted by what was being put forth as fact—the hyperbole, especially, of the innocence of his "victims." I began to figure Johnson at the intersection of an overwhelming amount of problematic rhetoric and policy regarding HIV and its specific racist-homophobic baggage, criminal justice and the prison industrial system, Black bodies and their exploitation in college sports, and the (non)conversation about consent in homosexual sex. Several poems in this collection use Johnson's case as their triggering subject.

"Paroxysm": Ezell Ford, 25, was shot and killed by police in Los Angeles on August 11, 2014. Ford suffered two fatal gunshot wounds—one in the back, where a muzzle imprint was left on his skin. In the sixth section ("The voice that is warning you constantly against"), the line "this incremental disappearance" paraphrases Dawn Lundy Martin in *DISCIPLINE* (New York: Nightboat, 2011).

ACKNOWLEDGMENTS

Thank you to the editors and readers of the following publications, in which versions of these poems appear.

Breakwater Review:	"A Statement from No One, Incorporated"
Callaloo:	"About a White City"
Columbia Poetry Review:	"Any Unkindness"
Eleven Eleven:	"Retrograde"
	"Untitled (We aint even posed to be here)"
Foglifter:	"Witness to the Woman I Am Not"
	"Nothing Was Ever Itself Only"
	"How to Keep It Down / Throw It Off / Defer until Asleep"
Jai-Alai:	"Exchange" (and "The Leak in This Old Building")
joINT.:	"Performing a Warped Masculinity en Route to the Metro"
	"Porch Smoke: An Implication in Three Acts"
	"On Self-Reliance"
Muzzle:	"Consent" (as "Sliver")
Obsidian:	"Slough"
	"Orientation"
The Offing:	"They Speak of the Body and One Sits Up Straight"
Phantom:	"Snowfall Throws Its Pretty Noise upon a Weary Sameness"
	"Necessary Room"
RHINO:	"Carolina Prayer"
The Shade Journal:	"The Fratricide"
The Tusculum Review:	"On Being a Grid One Might Go Off Of"
	"On Life as an Exercise in Preparing to Die"
Vinyl Poetry & Prose:	"Anesthesia Is a Country You Leave for America"
	"|p|l|e|a|s|"
Yalobusha Review:	"The Day _____ Died"
	"Gateway"

Selections from "Paroxysm" appear in the *Kenyon Review* and the *Iowa Review*.

Indecency was created in a dearth of sunlight, of personal interaction, and (often) of hope—which was not an easy terrain to return from. In addition to those folks who gave inspiration, feedback, encouragement, and edits, I must also thank those who checked in, refused to let me check out, made sure that I ate, kept me expressive, got me out of bed, and cared for me in other ways throughout this long project during which self-love was tenuous. Thank you to Aaron Coleman, Alison C. Rollins, Amber Jamilla Musser, Angel Nafis, Aricka Foreman, Avery Gallinat, Blair Johnson, Cheeraz Gormon, Claudia Rankine, CM Burroughs, Dawn Lundy Martin, Douglas Kearney, Felipe W. Martinez, francine j. harris, Hanif Abdurraqib, Jacqui Germain, Jayson P. Smith, Jonah Mixon-Webster, Khadijah Queen, KMA Sullivan, L. Lamar Wilson, Maurice Tracy, Pacia Anderson, Paul Legault, Patricia Smith, Rickey Laurentiis, Ronaldo V. Wilson, Saeed Jones, Shine Goodie, Steven Thrasher, Tafisha Edwards, Timothy Donnelly, and Treasure Shields Redmond. Thanks also to Kathleen Finneran, David Schuman, Edward McPherson, and the MFA at Washington University in St. Louis.

To Coffee House Press and to my editor Erika Stevens: thank you for taking a chance on this one, and for helping this dream to materialize in front of me.

To my teachers Mary Jo Bang and Carl Phillips: I wish for the work to be a testament to your care, devotion, and incredible patience. Thank you.

To my mentor and friend Phillip B. Williams: none of us deserves how much you give a damn, but thank you endlessly for it, and for making this collection happen.

To my family: your belief in me continues to be the greatest gift. To my momma: I am overwhelmed with the insufficiency of words. I love you. Thank you.

LITERATURE
is not the same thing as
PUBLISHING

Coffee House Press began as a small letterpress operation in 1972 and has grown into an internationally renowned nonprofit publisher of literary fiction, essay, poetry, and other work that doesn't fit neatly into genre categories.

Coffee House is both a publisher and an arts organization. Through our *Books in Action* program and publications, we've become interdisciplinary collaborators and incubators for new work and audience experiences. Our vision for the future is one where a publisher is a catalyst and connector.

Funder Acknowledgments

Coffee House Press is an internationally renowned independent book publisher and arts nonprofit based in Minneapolis, MN; through its literary publications and *Books in Action* program, Coffee House acts as a catalyst and connector—between authors and readers, ideas and resources, creativity and community, inspiration and action.

Coffee House Press books are made possible through the generous support of grants and donations from corporations, state and federal grant programs, family foundations, and the many individuals who believe in the transformational power of literature. This activity is made possible by the voters of Minnesota through a Minnesota State Arts Board Operating Support grant, thanks to the legislative appropriation from the arts and cultural heritage fund. Coffee House also receives major operating support from the Amazon Literary Partnership, the Jerome Foundation, The McKnight Foundation, Target Foundation, and the National Endowment for the Arts (NEA). To find out more about how NEA grants impact individuals and communities, visit www.arts.gov.

Coffee House Press receives additional support from the Elmer L. & Eleanor J. Andersen Foundation; the David & Mary Anderson Family Foundation; the Buuck Family Foundation; Fredrikson & Byron, P.A.; Dorsey & Whitney LLP; the Fringe Foundation; Kenneth Koch Literary Estate; the Knight Foundation; the Rehael Fund of the Minneapolis Foundation; the Matching Grant Program Fund of the Minneapolis Foundation; Mr. Pancks' Fund in memory of Graham Kimpton; the Schwab Charitable Fund; Schwegman, Lundberg & Woessner, P.A.; the U.S. Bank Foundation; VSA Minnesota for the Metropolitan Regional Arts Council; and the Woessner Freeman Family Foundation in honor of Allan Kornblum.

The Publisher's Circle
of Coffee House Press

Publisher's Circle members make significant contributions to Coffee House Press's annual giving campaign. Understanding that a strong financial base is necessary for the press to meet the challenges and opportunities that arise each year, this group plays a crucial part in the success of Coffee House's mission.

Recent Publisher's Circle members include many anonymous donors, Suzanne Allen, Patricia A. Beithon, the E. Thomas Binger & Rebecca Rand Fund of the Minneapolis Foundation, Robert & Gail Buuck, Claire Casey, Louise Copeland, Jane Dalrymple-Hollo, Mary Ebert & Paul Stembler, Kaywin Feldman & Jim Lutz, Chris Fischbach & Katie Dublinski, Sally French, Jocelyn Hale & Glenn Miller, the Rehael Fund-Roger Hale/Nor Hall of the Minneapolis Foundation, Randy Hartten & Ron Lotz, Dylan Hicks & Nina Hale, William Hardacker, Jeffrey Hom, Carl & Heidi Horsch, Amy L. Hubbard & Geoffrey J. Kehoe Fund, Kenneth Kahn & Susan Dicker, Stephen & Isabel Keating, Kenneth Koch Literary Estate, Cinda Kornblum, Jennifer Kwon Dobbs & Stefan Liess, Lenfestey Family Foundation, Sarah Lutman & Rob Rudolph, the Carol & Aaron Mack Charitable Fund of the Minneapolis Foundation, George & Olga Mack, Joshua Mack & Ron Warren, Gillian McCain, Mary & Malcolm McDermid, Sjur Midness & Briar Andresen, Maureen Millea Smith & Daniel Smith, Peter Nelson & Jennifer Swenson, Enrique Olivarez, Jr. & Jennifer Komar, Alan Polsky, Marc Porter & James Hennessy, Robin Preble, Alexis Scott, Ruth Stricker Dayton, Jeffrey Sugerman & Sarah Schultz, Nan G. & Stephen C. Swid, Patricia Tilton, Joanne Von Blon, Stu Wilson & Melissa Barker, Warren D. Woessner & Iris C. Freeman, Margaret Wurtele, and Wayne P. Zink & Christopher Schout.

For more information about the Publisher's Circle and other ways to support Coffee House Press books, authors, and activities, please visit www.coffeehousepress.org/support or contact us at info@coffeehousepress.org.

JUSTIN PHILLIP REED was born and raised in South Carolina. His work appears in the *African American Review, The Best American Essays, Callaloo,* the *Kenyon Review, Obsidian,* and elsewhere. He received an MFA in poetry from Washington University in St. Louis. The author of the chapbook *A History of Flamboyance* (YesYes Books 2016), he has received fellowships from the Cave Canem Foundation and the Conversation Literary Festival. He lives in St. Louis.

Indecency was designed by
Bookmobile Design & Digital Publisher Services.
Text is set in Perpetua.